Born to Love, Cursed to Feel

Samantha King

Andrews McMeel Publishing®

a division of Andrews McMeel Universal

To my Father, thank you for passing on your adoration of books, your unconditional love, support, and for standing by me through everything. I know I didn't always make it easy for you but I hope I make you proud. I just want you to know that my appreciation for you in my life is endless.

To Tasha and Frankie, thank you for embracing me and my creativity. You made sure I knew that being different wasn't a bad thing. It helped. Mom, I love you. To my family and friends, thank you for your kind words and support over the years.

To Reuben, you are nothing short of amazing. Thank you for encouraging me to put my work out into the world. I've grown so much with, and because of you. Your love and support have changed my life. I'm blessed to have you as my partner.

Perfect

You're a beautiful kind of madness
a misunderstood truth
O, the things they could learn from
the darkness that is hidden behind your eyes
So gifted, yet your talents are wasted
you gave up chasing dreams
Reality hit and you got a taste of failure
Cautious now about bearing your soul
For if others saw you fully exposed
they may not love you like they claim to
Time and experience have taught you to trust no one
Friends, lovers, and even family have forsaken you
You keep the shattered pieces of your heart in a box
Stitching, gluing, and staying up all night
trying to put it back together
Attempting to fill the void that was left
Moving from one man to the next
It seems no one can satisfy the appetite
for affection that you seek
Continually picking at old wounds
they never heal properly
You have no real home, too restless to stay in one place

You are reckless, selfish, stubborn, sometimes rude

You've bottled up the pain

of so much that has been done

When you're hurt

You close into yourself, shut down

You love attention and yet love being by yourself more

May God have mercy on your soul

For you are truly lost

Daily you fight your demons

Yet no one knows of that which you endure

You bear it alone, never speaking of it

You can blame the broken home from which you came

Or the environment that you grew up in

The people who tore you down so young

You can point the finger at those who have

whispered behind your back

They all have played a role in your development

But looking so deep into the past

will keep you from moving forward

You must love yourself more

than these people claim they do

Look at where you stand now

No one can know the things you have endured like you

You've never claimed to be perfect

Your flaws tell your story

There is no need to hide them

Eyes Open

The scary part is I knew exactly how bad
you were for me
and yet that didn't stop me
from loving you

One

I don't look for you in anything
For in everything you are
Where I am, you exist
In each breath, every smile
and even in moments of pain
your presence resides
I am cloaked in your spirit, utterly submerged in you
Reality so beautiful, something I can see and feel
You're someone I believe in
How was I so fortunate to come across such bliss?
Kissed by Heaven's favor, perhaps
Spoke it into existence, maybe
You and I were always made for this moment
Fate may have brought us together, but we chose to stay

Unyielding

It's been years and your life still has no room for me
I write myself in where I can

Wrong Mark

Do you ever think of me in a prolonged agony?

Does your soul search for me while you rest?

Have you forgotten my eyes or the fire they set ablaze when you gazed into them?

I miss you

I sit here lost, genuinely yearning to know what you're doing and where you are

O sweet Cupid, what have you done?

I call foul play here

How is it I came to love a man who now feels like a stranger?

Good-bye

I thought I would be devastated without you
I was waiting for everything to rip apart
The sky didn't come crashing down
Air still flows through my lungs
Blood surges through my veins
I thought I would lie down in surrender
I didn't give my heart enough credit
I sit here waiting for it
The realization that you are a part of my Life no more
I've wrapped my mind around the notion
It's possible I already cried enough
Perhaps the year and a half spent trying to make sense of all this
has finally drained me
Maybe, just maybe, I always knew I deserved better, but was too
afraid to accept it
I feel as if I should mourn us
Except I sit here relieved
I gave you my all
and took the loss that even that wasn't enough
Maybe, just maybe, you were never meant to be mine no matter
how hard I loved you
You broke me in ways that I've never experienced before and if I'm

wise enough

will not allow myself to endure again

I no longer think of you as often or long for you at night

There are moments where you are missed

that I cast into the light of your negligence

and allow it to burn away and die

I hungered for Love, your Love, and starved

No worries, I carry no hate in my heart for you

I want no parts of you to linger long here

You weren't ready for the Love I could give

Now I have a different plan in mind

Defeat

I've withered in your shadow

My love no longer grows in leaps and bounds

It is not rooted

There is no nourishment to soak in

I am left ravenous for your attention

Some kind of passion, a simple touch

The air between the sweet words that are whispered

None of it is given and yet I crave so much

You know it

Yet stand tall and resolute with your back to me

You stopped adoring me the way you used to

My mind has registered this

My heart just won't accept it

It believes that if I keep trying

one day we'll make it

somewhere, deep down though, I know this isn't true

In time you will simply be diminished to the man who broke me to

the point that I was forced to face myself

Forever you will live between

the black and white of these pages

Despite that, your love fell somewhere in the gray

I am somehow more of myself now

This has been no mild transition
My back was broken to please you
My mind strained
My heart tested and persevered
in ways unknown to it before
There is no satisfaction in this stunted growth
I've imprisoned myself to doing my best to love a man
who can't love me back the way I need him to
The way I deserve
You've always had the knowledge of my dreams
You just decided not to be a part of them

Hooked

Your detachment is my elixir

I want to inject the essence of you into my veins

and get lost in the quakes of your past

High off the levels you've been to

that I've never reached

Let me be your shadow

always present, always watching, always listening

You are my addiction

So peaceful, so enticing, I'm borderline obsessed

I want to know you, no, I need to know

How is it that all my Life has led up to this moment?

Your eyes are piercing

 I don't shrink or hide

Light me on fire with them

You've already destroyed my mind

might as well take my body with it

My mystery, my enchantment, how are you so many things to me

and yet nothing?

Vow of Silence

I spoke out of fear and you ignored me
I spoke out of pain and you didn't listen
I spoke out of love and you walked away
So now I speak of nothing

Karma

She's been watching me
She's been patient
Lying dormant in anticipation
She's waited for this moment
I feel her breath on my neck
Forgiven but not forgotten
My time must be paid in full
Suffering has not yet ended
It has only pooled, waiting to drown me in my shame
It knows all, despite the trails that have been covered
The countless names of offenses
that never made it to the ear of their victim
I have not always been good,
but he has made me want to be more
The depths of love I feel for him cannot be uttered
There simply is not justification in words for this
Not this time, this time it is something far different
So rare that I tread softly
in fear that if I approach too fast it will flee
She knows this
I've caught her lurking around the corners of my joy
The weight of her presence unhinging my sanity

She's a sign that a storm is inevitable

I'm down on my knees begging

"Please don't do this to me"

No form of redemption is enough

A simple explanation of I was young and dumb

will not save me

I'm starting to wonder if my paranoia

is punishment enough

Yet I know better

My debt must be paid in full

Karma, release me

Woke

I get it, doing what you can

to not think about the girl you can't have

The one who told you her fears

like you were going to be the last one to hear it

She only gives herself in pieces

rare and very few have her in her uninhibited form

With you words came easy

but were never really needed

Sometimes you lie awake at night

hoping that she will call and say she misses you

It doesn't happen

She never really quite said the right thing

something always held her back

It was written on her face

There's no relief to what you feel

For as much as she is your reality she plagues your dreams as well

So, eyes open, you conjure thoughts of her

allow fantasies to create what reality won't

Eyes closed, she's right there,

but no matter how much you reach for her

there is no feeling of her face against your hand

You can't say you Love her yet

One day though you would like to find that you do
To feel her touch, her warmth
her relentless need for you
A dream unattainable
You wake up from it every time she says his name
The sober realization that she is owned by no one
and yet chained to a man you've heard of
but never met
What does he do for her?
Is it him she dreams of?
Does he crave her the way you do?
Would he understand the persistent desire to be there when she
needs it?
She cried today; today you saw her cry
You watched the tears roll down her face
As the mask of her strength melted before you
You wanted to stay, but had already begun to say good-bye
She grasped your hand, tried to anchor you to the lie, but you had
already seen the truth
No matter how good you were
or how much you desired her
she would be his till she decided otherwise

Caring for someone who loves another is no easy task

You found the courage to walk away and not look back

Those tears may follow you for some time

but like her will become a distant memory

Life is about the choices we make

the moments we don't see coming

and the strength to do what's best for ourselves

despite how much it may hurt

You were brave enough to wake up

now don't go back to sleep

Sweet Deception

It all seemed so perfect
I guess lies are that way
They wait until you're entangled in them
Wrapped in their beauty
and the minute you start to believe they're real
They rip apart all the hope you had left

Anguish

I went to the dark part of my mind
Put one foot on the shovel and dug you up
I needed to look one more time, just one more glance
My mistake was thinking it was really over
because once free
you decided to wreak havoc on the rest of my mind
Making it dark too

Vital

I want to be singed by your passion
Release me of this existence and
reincarnate me into the air you breathe
Let me be what sustains you
Leaving a trace of my imprint
pumping through your veins

Home

His dirty socks and shoes on the floor

My hair clogging up the drain

Clothes scattered everywhere and the loud tapping

of the typewriter I got him for his birthday

I was once alone and then this chaos ensued

that we now call a home

Despite whatever complaints I may have

I wouldn't want it any other way or with anyone else

Partner in Crime

Friend, let my eyes be the guide to your beauty
that you have yet to discover
Let my heart be your safe haven
When your world begins to darken and storms
wash away the essence of your faith
Let my fingers entwine with yours
serving as reassurance that there is nothing
that you will ever have to face alone

Life's Student

There is growth in pain
You just have to find the lesson and learn it

Ghosts of New York

I would like to think that they all have their own stories
But we never ask, we don't even know their names
Or what has brought them to their knees and humbled them
enough to sleep on the floor of a station
Or sit on a train all night long just to have
somewhere warm to sleep
They are gawked at
people will leave their presence to avoid the smell
but they have nowhere to wash their bodies
On those days when you've argued
with your boss or a friend,
something didn't go your way
and you think you have it bad,
They are walking, breathing, living evidence
that someone out there truly has it worse
We've made ourselves so cold, so immune
that we've taken the humanity out
of what's happening in front of us
So yes, I would like to believe that
when I give them that dollar
they aren't going to use it
to put a needle in their arm

and if they should, who am I to judge?

Maybe when you're already that low

all there is left to live for is chasing that high

Thinking Out Loud

So self-destructive I'm waiting for the implosion
For the Universe's infinite wisdom to cave in my chest and abolish
all my fears
To be driven so deep into the possibilities
that I am blinded by the light
Until all I can do is close my eyes
and be forced to once again dream genuinely
Before the day of naysayers and doubts
I'm in the stairwell hiding from the people
hiding from the noise
Can they see my insecurities as vividly as I do?
Do they possess that kind of vision?
Or are they so lost in their own self-turmoil that they don't even
notice I'm defeated, depleted
A remnant of a dreamer gone mad
A hopeless romantic who hasn't been fed
An artist starving for Life, to Live

Justice

Living, but not really living

Breathing, but not really savoring every precious breath

Believing, but at the same time doubting

That this pain will ever cease to exist

Overwhelming doses of emotion

Can someone prescribe me something so I can go numb?

I need a moment

Something more than these

unrelenting episodes of sorrow and anguish

Is there no joy left for me?

Will there ever be a moment where I can truly smile?

Will there ever be a time where I won't attempt to

imagine your face?

I'd give anything to have a second chance

To give you a second thought

I'm engulfed in what could have been

Consumed in it so much

That the present all seems like a blur

I've done many things

That I will choose to forget

But this is by far my worst regret

I cannot change what has been done

No matter how many stars I wish upon

So I'll go on

Smiling, but not really smiling

Loving, but not really loving

Living, but not really living

Comfort

When I hit that wall, and I am going to hit it

As I'm lying on the floor consumed by despair

don't try and pick me up

don't whisper words of comfort

Don't tell me it's going to be ok

Let me be in this moment where I think it's not

Lie beside me and let me find hope in the comfort of your presence

Let me deal with my thoughts and fears

I will eventually reprimand myself for indulging in such an

emotion for so long

I will want to get up and keep moving forward

Until then, let me lie here and let the salt of my tears sting the

wounds you can't see

Until I'm ready, let me be

I have to heal myself

Fool Me Twice

I took a risk by reinvesting myself

I took an even bigger one when I began to care

But I tightened the knot of the noose around my neck

When I began to Love you again

You kicked the chair out from under me

So I didn't even have to jump

Canvas

Forlorn, lost

I thought I would have it by now

I'm somewhere between

"Is this really my life?" and "Where am I right now?"

I measured who I was supposed to be

against the picture that you painted

Now I'm stuck with this brush, my chaotic thoughts,

and this canvas

I never wanted perfect, I just wanted happy

I'm still figuring out what that looks like

Moving On

Your nighttime fool

your daytime Lover

I should have been off this road

about four text messages and three missed calls ago

Sitting in the dark pondering the thought of you

Dear Sandman, why have you yet to come?

I need this slumber

The pain has finally overrun me

So low I think the ground

has become envious of my position

If you no longer desired my Love

then you simply could have told me

There was no need to drag me along

and punish me this way

My friends are exhausted

from the relentless phone calls of sobs and silence

The "help me" look that has invaded my face

and the absence of who I was before us

Who has seemed to be taken over

by a situation that simply should have not been endured but ended

This isn't some timeless romance, just a tragedy

I'm done letting you have that kind of control

I'm no longer waiting for the ending

I'm writing one without you

Old School

Don't you miss the days when being in a relationship meant there
was no competition?
Where separation was a last resort
after all other means had been exhausted
When you didn't wait up all night
creeping through social media
to know what your partner was doing
Love letters were handwritten and saved
They knew your favorite candy
and laughter was in abundance
Are we all so focused on not getting hurt
that we'd destroy another to spare ourselves?
Do you remember the days when sex
wasn't bartered and women weren't so easily subjected?
Do you remember when "I love you" meant something?
Did those days ever exist?

Other Woman

It's 3 a.m.

My phone's going off

He's on his way

I should be sleeping

rather than waiting anxiously for him

It can't be helped though

He's my addiction

and when he's gone too long I'm in withdrawal

A self-inflicted agony

I let him in

He never stays long

regardless of how much I plead with him to

He already has a home where he belongs

I was just a refuge for what he wouldn't share with her

This week she and I finally met

She had caught me staring in his direction

I was in shock

The knowledge of her was always in my possession

but since I had never seen her

I acted as if she was nonexistent, somewhat irrelevant to my life

To cover up for the intrusion my eyes made

he introduced me as an old friend

I went along with the story he fabricated out of thin air
She believed him
My eyes scanned her curvy frame
They stopped at her protruding stomach
She noticed then gushed that she was 5 months
"It's a boy"
No wonder she was glowing
She was truly beautiful
I felt the bile rise in the back of my throat
She insisted that she get my information
so when the baby shower was held I could come
If she only knew that my info had been across his lips
and held within his hands
After we departed he texted
"That was a close one, good job though, babe. See you later on"
I cried the tears that because of her ignorance she would never shed
To go on like this
would truly be the cause of my demise
At midnight he texted me
At 1 a.m. he called
At 2 a.m. he wrote again
At 3 a.m. I turned off my phone

Role Reversal

Let's trade places
You wait up all night
for a phone call that never comes
You can fall asleep to the empty nothingness
instead of my voice
You can feel like you're giving your all for nothing
and wake up alone
No text, no call, no indication that you were thought of
No apology, just empty promises
Words of sentiment that lack the real affection
Try feeling like you're compromising yourself once again
to receive nothing in return
You can open up your heart and have nothing fill it
Wonder every morning
why you're even doing this
and then shed the tears I'll never see
You can watch me walk away
But there is no need to switch sides
to see that happen

Sober

The end came quicker than your climax
You should have pulled out
Or maybe I should have listened
'Cause while my heart was beating for you
the head that was penetrating
was the only one functioning
Your refuge was always the pink, candy-coated satisfaction in
between my legs
Not my words, not my soul, not everything I gave
But simply the intoxicating ecstasy
that came from the undeniable connection
our bodies have when brought together
Inches and inches of skin cascading over
the pulsating rhythm that
infiltrated the walls of my hesitance
You knew my weakness before my lips separated
to divulge my surrender
I guess you saw in me
what you've seen in yourself for years
I really need to stop, but can't
Staring into your eyes stirs an unfamiliar feeling
that I can't object

There isn't a better sight than your eyes when you smile

But after you've departed I feel incomplete

The void so colossal

I swear only you can fill it

But you were never truly mine

My love was borrowed

Only given during the circumstances that were convenient for you

Never when I needed it

I refuse to continue to retreat to the place where I lost my sense

of morality

Clinging to the hope of a feeling that only exists when our

bodies meet

Creating the kind of release that no drug-induced state of mind

could ever make us reach

I'm done with feeling like I'm on top of it all

To then crash with every false step taken

I've taken control of my destiny

I like being sober

My Truth

I lost everything trying to do right
My sanity, my hope, and eventually
the will to keep trying
What was shameful wasn't the way you loved me
but the way I loved you
You could never match what I gave
and deep down I always knew it

Relapse

Lying in her bed she thought it was over
The cold sweats had stopped months ago
She hadn't craved it for weeks
With each passing day
the hours no longer seemed so endless
Just when she thought she had broken free
she was sinking under again
At first there was no desire to stray
No yearning for the familiar gratification
of rising so high above the burdens
that the world heaved onto her shoulders
That beautiful paradise, that intoxicating escape
She got a taste of that o so compelling sensation
and didn't realize she was under
until he was penetrating all of her forces
It was an all too familiar scene
Remembering the crash is hard
when you're knee-deep in the haze of ecstasy

She awoke alone
to the feeling of defeat
It wasn't worth it
It never was

Tomorrow

How I allowed myself to get here
Is still a question I have yet to answer
The walls cry out his name
The shirt that he left behind
that I am now wearing
is drenched in his scent
His side of the bed is unbearably vacant
everything reminds me of him
It's almost as if I'm being punished
This is exactly why I should leave
Yet I sit and wait
for a man I can't call my own
A man who says he sees us together in the future
But can't commit to me today
It's been over a year now
I've come to realize
I deserve better
Giving in, succumbing to his needs and desires
is a full-time job all its own
For which I put in overtime
and yet I go unpaid
I allowed myself to be enslaved by my so-called feelings

for a man unworthy of my time and effort

One day I'm going to walk away and never look back

At least that's what I keep telling myself

My phone rings, it's him

He's coming over

I want to fuss

tell him it's either something more or he can leave

But somehow his smile soothes me

Once in his grasp his touch feeds my need for affection

I fall asleep in his arms

Thinking maybe I'll have the strength to leave

Tomorrow

A Stolen Lesson

You stole my voice
How could I let you?
Silencing my own thoughts and dreams
Because they were so loud they drowned you out
You stole my time
How could I give it so easily?
Hours were toiled over what you were doing
whether or not you really loved me
Minutes were spent in your presence
while it was only for seconds
that I was actually happy
You stole my pride
I became a fool, your own personal jester
For I would rather see you smile
than taste the bitterness of my tears
when I was without you
You stole my love
Why me? Why you? Why now?
I didn't know I was giving it
Until it was already gone
Even when my mind was screaming
"You know better"

I may have suffered but in the end have won

For you had to take all these things

And now are left with nothing

While I have learned my lesson

Behind Brown Eyes

It'd be ignorant of me
To try and sit here and discuss your pain
Pretend I have the solution
As if this was a simple problem
and not the destruction of your heart once again
I'm sending my regards
I simply can't bear to watch you fade into your grief
Stiff, cold, too far away for me to reach
I want to see the joy that was once in your eyes
The thirst for adventure
That hunger for life
I don't know if I ever told you
that you made me better
And although I don't say much
I've always been around
just in case you need me
Pain is inevitable
It's how you choose to heal that matters
I apologize that the desecration of your
bountiful optimism was so swift
laid out for others to see
Don't give him the satisfaction

of dwelling on words of sentiment

Those were clearly lies

Actions will always trump pretty words

I won't offend you by

simply stating that in time you'll heal

My friend, all I will say is

That I love you

And until the shards of your heart are

stitched back together, fully revived

I have no problem with letting you borrow mine

9—5

Time ticks away

Screaming its objection

That the hours should pass so leisurely

Till I should be with you again

It is only the passing of such that could tear us apart

Good or bad, whatever the day should bring

I will never mind

As long as you are always the conclusion

Dear...

You're the poem I couldn't finish

The journey I should have never started

I saw tragedy in our ending

My pen bled its heart out trying to change it

But you were the fight I didn't want to lose

The addiction I didn't want to quit

Yet there was only one of us holding on

I wasn't attached to the man you are

But the one you could be

I tried to build where there was no foundation

Create a fairy tale on blank pages

But some stories need not be told, let alone written

You'll read my words and won't be moved

Your arrogance will not soften

You won't be changed

Your heart, if you should have one,

will not bend or break

The worst part of it all

Is this poem is about you

and you'll never even know it

Breaking Point

I'm sorry is no longer a healing balm

It won't happen again is just another lie

I see the remorse on your face

I can just no longer sympathize

You've drained me of whatever ability I had left

to dig a little deeper and

believe this was worth saving

I won't be staying tonight

I won't be coming back tomorrow

You can keep your watered-down promises of forever

Insanity

If I'm losing my mind now
it's because I've allowed myself to believe
I can stand tall in something that's sinking
without going under

Confession

I hate you wouldn't quite do it
I forgive you isn't quite my speed
I regret meeting you would be a lie
The best thing for me
was removing you from my life
That, I am sure of

In the Lonely Hour

We yearn so badly to be healed

We let anyone in

We cram them into what small space we have left

Hoping they have good intentions

Fin

I feel sick

Completely exposed, vulnerable

I have never showed a truer form of myself

than when in your arms

It is displayed on my face

In the increasing beat of my heart

My mind abhors you

For she has yet to find peace since you arrived

My eyes simply shun the sight of you

It sends me down a relentless spiral of flashbacks

Can you see the memories that once brought me joy now cause

utter pain?

Do you torture me on purpose?

I have never hated nor loved you more

It is not that I regret

what we once meant to each other

It's just the days that I no longer reminisce over us

couldn't come sooner

December

People always ask
When did I know
It could have been when I woke up
and watched you rest peacefully beside me
or all those times I learned how much we're alike
But it was when we had that fight
I wanted to cry and laugh hysterically
Guess that's insanity
We didn't leave
We sat in silence
The reason behind it all so small
I knew then just how much I loved you
And as you crossed over and merely
wrapped me in your arms
I knew just how much you loved me

Double-Edged Sword

I can't get back the hours, the effort,
or that little piece of me that believed in you
You would think I'm the one who suffered here
but that's only 'cause you haven't figured out what you lost

Gone

Every move you made you were allowed to

I saw it coming

I didn't move out of the way of disaster

I stood in it

Taking in the chaos around me

I refused to bend

The pain was internal

But I had to withstand this, you

You couldn't say good-bye

So I collected my things and moved on without you

His Sorrow

The notes on his heart never manifest to be heard
The dreams that were once his love for life
now rest soundly with his fears
Nothing tastes as sweet
The colors have lost their radiance
Life seems like it's dwindling away
Just grains of sand lost in an hourglass
The hours of contemplation
and strain perceptible on his face
Hair disheveled, thoughts scattered
No need to breathe
To savor this mild existence is now meaningless
There are no tears shed for the broken pieces of a man's heart
Good guys finish last too frequently
They both said I love you
He was the only one who meant it

Unforgiven

I've tried to think of the words to tell you
Create a masterpiece of my pain
Paint it against the walls of your mind
So you can't forget what your negligence has manifested
I strove for perfection
A compilation of words that could invoke the emotion
My heart bleeds when the sound of your voice reaches my ears
The conflict between it and my mind
For I am old enough to know
But young enough not to care that I knew you were no good for me
I wanted to make your blue sky gray
Let the clouds shower upon you
The tears shed over the moments when I realized
That you never cared as much as I did
What I desired, what I yearned for you to see
Can simply be understood by me saying
You broke the best part of me
And no, you're not forgiven

Solace

I consistently neglect you

attempt to replace you with others

Yet you always allow me to return

The yearning in the bottom of my stomach

That notion like something is missing

can be filled with no one but you

I try to deny it, but you give me purpose

Without you I'm nothing

No cliché intended, I mean it

When my face is stained with tears

you are there to console me

When my heart is filled with joy

you are there to relish it

You know of all my secrets and fears

All the while you have never judged me

You'll let me pour out my heart

in the early hours of the morning

You never complain of my repetitive mistakes

but serve as a witness to all the ways

I've learned not to find Love

My Confidant, My Best Friend, the Essence of my Soul

Poetry, you are now and will always be the better part of me

Retrospect

I blamed you so long for who I became

It was much easier than facing that I allowed myself to become that

Quicksand

I wrote my last letter
Left it on the bed
Took it all in once more
Dropped my keys on the table
Unhinged what doubts were left
Then I walked away without looking back
A memory of how I got here
evoked with each step taken
The hours spent waiting up for you to get home
The countless mornings I awoke
to find myself still alone
The never-ending pleas of "please just listen"
fell upon ears that weren't ready to hear it
Casual conversations led to arguments of
"Where have you been?" and "What are we?"
My hopes for "us" began to weigh me down
It seemed no matter what was done
all that was said
the harder I fought the faster I began to sink
Paralyzed, submerged in my fears
I went from blaming me to you to me again
to coming to terms with the fact

that just because you Love someone
doesn't mean you're supposed to be with them

Perception

I lost myself
Weighed down by the emotions
that chained me to your existence
I found when I unlocked what bound me
that I felt different
A smile no longer seemed so painful
with you not around
The good moments could be enjoyed even if not shared
Every second wasn't given to the thought of you
I realize now how much I was killing me loving you
You may not have noticed
the pain that your uncertainty caused
The walls your lies built up
The fabrications you told that made me hope
to only then shatter on the reality of who you are
I loved you with my heart
But I forgot to do it with my eyes open
Lesson learned

Untitled

I died a thousand deaths

Trying to get you to Love me once

You never did

There's a part of me that didn't survive "Us"

Peace of Mind

It's impossible to write down every emotion
that has been stirred
Write an obituary for every tear that has fallen
Meeting its end upon my face
To give a voice to all the thoughts
existing solely to taunt me
Screaming their position, debating their importance
Insisting, even pleading for a moment of focus
"Solve me before you move on to the next"
Silently waiting for action to be taken on their behalf
Hoping their simple existence isn't in vain
This isn't where I want to be
Nor do I know where I am going
Hopefully I'll find my peace on the way

Peril

The walls are talking
and all they are saying is your name
Fighting through the downpour
of the recent news you gave
I am drenched in your indifference
Shivering within your disdain
Cowering from the thunderous presence of your doubts
Awaiting the sun of what was once
our happiness to peek out
Offer some light
I've never been the one to put much faith in hope
Yet I sit here now hoping that in the midst of all this
You don't forget that at one point in time
the radiance stemming from our joy was overwhelming
The flirtatious laughter contagious
But it was the Love
So passionate, so raw
It was bold enough to make even the greatest of Loves wonder
How we fell into this so gracefully
I sit here, spurned by your absence
Wearing your shirt
I slide into our bed on your side
I won't be getting much sleep

Reconsider

Messages can be deleted

Little keepsakes tossed away

Yet the memories won't offer me a moment of peace

From the torment of constantly seeing your face

My lips refusing to forget

the sensation felt against yours

They move trying to force what needs to be said out

My heart has betrayed me

My hand mourns the loss of its partner

And my eyes try to be strong

But sympathetically shed what they hope will be a release

Alleviation from the weight of the realization

That I was wrong

Things went too far and despite the fact that I could see it climbing

I stopped but only before something else pushed me forward

Was it fear, my insecurities, my past, was I trying to save you from me

Or was it a combination of it all?

Who knows?

All you ever wanted was to gain the knowledge of

What made my smile fade

What made me laugh less

What stole my glow

I hid it all from you
I'll take responsibility for that

Fraud

While you were claiming to protect me from others
Someone should have protected me from you

Try

Is there no humanity left?

Does there not reside in the hearts of any one person

some compassion?

I know you think ill of my actions

I just do not know how to proceed

To somehow pretend that everything is alright

When it isn't

The words no longer form so easily

around the thought of you

So nothing that escapes me comes out right

I sit silently awaiting my soul to awaken

For something entirely magnificent to happen

To make this fine

It hasn't, dare I say it ever will?

There is no comfort rooted in the sound of your voice

Where I readily used to take refuge

I just can't quite figure out how to mend the bonds that have

become unhinged

Mask the hesitation to once again walk alongside you

into whatever form of danger or happiness

that lurked along the road

I searched to find where it had all gone wrong

Leaving me to wonder, are we to just start again?

Act as if there wasn't an adventurous past that existed

Don't hate me

You believe I'm not trying, but each day is a struggle

My forgiveness isn't going to be instantaneous

Your betrayal wasn't expected

Anything worth working at takes time

So if you choose to stay

Have no expectations from which to fall, disappointed

If you choose to go

I will respect your wishes

Just know that I did in fact try

Intimacy

I rather you fall in love with my naked soul than my naked body

I am more than breasts and ass

I am a sensation

I am to be felt without being touched

I am to be understood without being seen

The Endless Struggle

I write what I can't say

I weep for these lost emotions

These voiceless, unclaimed soldiers that go to battle every day

Only to lose their lives spilling out onto my cheeks

So many casualties have been laid to rest upon my pillowcase

What should bring my head solace is now a graveyard for

abandoned feelings

I sit up and work over and over in my mind

Is there any logic to it all?

For that to truly exist emotion would need to cease

I struggle with the war that's continuing inside me as we speak

Defined by impulsions, confined

Inescapable Truth

Words escape me now

in the time that I need them most

What is there left to say that hasn't already been said?

What path hasn't been laid before our feet to try?

Trapped within the ruins of what this once was

We're somewhere under the rubble

Your name has been spoken

from my lips a million times

You haven't noticed

You feel I don't listen

I'm just waiting for something profound to be said to make the

void stop growing

No longer your muse

my value in your eyes has depleted

You seek the benefit of a love worth having

I see the benefit of one worth keeping

When did we become so mean?

Name-calling, finger-pointing, ignoring

I'll type it out and still won't be able to capture the sorrow felt

From watching in horror all that we are becoming

Long Distance

My fingers stroke a dirty screen

Aching to feel his skin beneath them

I lay next to it pretending I'm really there beside him

We stare at each other

knowing we have other things to do

The energy so magnetic we delay leaving

I'm living and breathing here

but my heart is so far away

I yearn to hear his voice, see his face

To know he is safe and well

The fact that we dream under the same sky

should bring comfort

But a sunset is just not the same through a picture

Our moments are shared and stored

but my desire is to feel them completely

I would gladly weather any storm

if he were literally next to me

For how can I shun the wind and the rain

while I sit with my Blessing

They have their purpose in Life

and I believe his is to love me as I love him

For now until what I want comes to be

I'll appreciate that God thought fondly enough to have our paths
cross and be so intertwined
That I get to laugh, love, smile, and be weird
Even if for now it's through a screen

Love

Are you tired of me saying your name?

Are you ashamed that I declare you so often when most times it

seems that it was in vain?

Are you mad that I am not more cautious when I play your card?

Or are you just tired of watching me

stuff my pockets with the broken pieces of my heart?

Remnants

There comes a point where there aren't any tears left

When we have lost what we've held dear

all that's left are the memories

They taunt us, reminding us of the happiness that we once felt

Awakening the pain that isn't easily released

One day, when we've found closure and the scar tissue covers the
wounds left

The memories will no longer seem like punishment, but serve as
evidence of our resilience

Gamble

We give people multiple chances
hoping that they'll change
I don't know if it speaks less of them
for taking advantage
Or less of us for refusing
to accept who they are

The Beginning

The beauty of first dates and first kisses
Of "I miss you" and "No, you hang up first"
Of staring into each other's eyes
and then laughing for no reason
Trying hard not to admit that the tingling sensation
in your stomach wasn't just unexpected but exquisite

Secret

The name you'll whisper but won't say out loud

The call you'll make in the middle of the night

The hour matters not to you

As you twist words around and around

draining them of their sweetness

All to lie in between sheets

I am the one you cry out for when you're alone

when no one is listening

I hate you

You've made me a detested secret

I'm ashamed that I crawled into the closet

that you built for me

Believing I deserve no more than that

I've marked the days

that I allowed myself to be so stupid

It may take double that or more

for me to forgive myself

For you, I feel no grace or empathy

I felt for you with what I had

and you took the best of me

Sufficient enough to attain, be consumed in, overwhelmed by

Yet never good enough to be claimed

I hope when you open the door
to find that I'm no longer there
That for one second you sit where I sat and contemplate
whether you ever deserved someone like me

Over

It became too much
The arguments became louder, the fights often
Trust diminished over time and lines were crossed
Drunken phone calls and bad decisions
It wasn't from a lack of trying but a lack of respect
Bridges turned to ashes
No need to mourn them

Hindsight

I screamed, you didn't hear me

I walked away, you didn't chase

I've found that our value lies not in what's spoken between us but

in all the things your actions say

I've cried more than I've smiled

I've lost more than I've gained

I'm tired of sacrificing but no big fuss 'cause you won't even notice

what's happened

until it's already too late

Progress

So often we are defined by what we've done

and the mistakes we've made

For once I would like to be

Measured by the steps I took today

Rather than the footprints of yesterday

Haunted

I'd give anything to steal a glance of your happiness
Feel your fingers interlocked in mine
My love for you hasn't died or subsided
I tried to bury it deep somewhere
but it finds me
I'm living in a constant state of flashbacks
The past so vivid, leaking into my present
I can't get away from you
One minute you're here, the next minute I can't even reach out to
touch you
I know it's wrong to linger for so long on this feeling
You're not coming back
Is my regret for not keeping you so strong that your existence
haunts me?

Last Leg

The power of words
Emotions that hang in the air
The space between what is said
and what hasn't quite made it to the surface
Time's significance lived out in stolen moments
Lost in the abyss of negligence
The climb seems more strenuous
Life has upped the ante, there's more at stake
We strive for a better understanding
yet rest on the platforms of our own ignorance
Too stubborn to truly admit
that there may be something to what is being said
A possibility that our own sides
aren't the only right path
The haze between our perceptions of what is
and what could be has grown as thick as the tension
Helplessly feeling around for some
common ground to hold on to
Afraid of what will happen should this bond crumble
We try to build bridges but they break
So I watch from a distance
Again, admonished to be simply an admirer
There was once a time where we were truly happy

Sacrifice

The war between my mind and my heart
has been the biggest destruction of my peace
To think I turned the better parts of me
against one another all for the sake of keeping you

Disorder

My room is a mess, my life is cluttered

I'm obsessed with love from an indifferent lover

I wait in anticipation for a revelation that isn't coming

I don't know what I want more

Unconditional love or just something to stop the longing

Foolish

He was never really mine
and in truth he was never really hers either
The only thing he belonged to was his desires
and anyone who would fulfill them

Abandonment Issues

I always wondered why it was so easy
For people to leave
What I should have questioned was
Why I wanted so badly for them to stay

Revelation

I've learned to face my demons
I'm just learning everybody can't handle them

False Hope

Stop waiting for it to make sense

Stop using that as an excuse to leave the door open

It's not closure that you're seeking

It's this hope that despite what's gone wrong

everything can go back to normal

Pause

I want to press stop
but can't seem to find the button
The words are stuck on replay in my mind
What's being said is loud and clear
It's what isn't that is resonating
We went too far, we should have stopped
Pain met me last night and left with me this morning
Confusion decided to tag along
My mind is two seconds from imploding
"It's not that serious"
So why do I feel so slighted?
I prefer not to dwell on this
but the tears shed from our fight haunt me
The realization that their existence mattered not
is a weight I didn't plan to carry
I was wrong, you were wrong
Fingers can be pointed but both our hands are filthy
Voices were raised to tune the other out
Points were spoken in vain
since our mouths were moving
While our ears weren't really listening
We could have stopped, we should have stopped

Ruins

Collecting memories like they're artifacts

If I keep enough then maybe I can build my heart back

Or at the very least remember why we went wrong

Clarity

Maybe I'm not as okay as I want to believe

Maybe those broken pieces I keep denying

are attracting the wrong souls

Who linger way too long trying to take away

whatever light I have left and I let them

Maybe it's time to fess up that it's not them, it's me

Devotion

May your heart never break

But if it should I'll be here to pick up the pieces

May your soul never grow weary

But if it should

may the light of my soul rejuvenate yours

May your legs never give out from under you

But if they should

I will carry you wherever you need to go

May your hand never feel lonely

But if it should, my friend,

know that my hand is always yours to hold

War Zone

I continue to fight a losing battle
Praying this tribulation will cease
Or at least that I will have the strength to sustain it
Each day I wake and wonder
if this is really love or
am I just not brave enough to leave
Rapid-fire shots, words like venom
I yearn for the peace of mind from a smile
or the comfort of arms to cuddle in
The warmth in your eyes has faded
I'm not fighting anymore
Loving myself is already enough of an uphill battle

No Stars in Brooklyn

We have the past, the present, and we are the future

We are history's notes

and someone's dream comes to fruition

We are ambition, We are the Hustle, We Set the Bar

But, O God, what I would give

to look up and see the stars

To be in awe of Your magnificence

Your celestial beauty painted

against the canvas of the sky

In that moment I would know how small I am

my life lacking no significance due to my size in the greater scheme

of things because it must be done

I'm a little light walking these streets

When my time has come to pass

and if I should be worthy of Your gates,

Lord, please cast my Soul into the sky

and let someone look up hoping to find me

Futile

Chased from room to room on delicate feet

Clusters of words try to fight through the sobs

Eyes once sweet and enticing

The brightest sort of welcome

Now look steely through mine

Almost demand silence

Hands tug hands

Pull and push

Anything to stop the departure

Crushed

I listened in utter shock and disbelief
The mouth that kissed me the night before
Was now rapidly bringing me to tears
Not missing a beat as he ripped me apart
I kept telling myself through it all
That he loved me
Until I couldn't anymore

Reality Check

You were merely my creation
A testament to my inability to accept the truth
I ignored the bruises
In my mind there was painted an amazing picture
of a man you never manifested to be
All that's left of you now are the scars on me

Prince Charming

I rushed to fill in the gaping holes

that I didn't even notice the foundation was giving way

I built and rebuilt and fixed what I could of our home

I was the only one fixing it

You watched, you criticized

and when it came down on me

You walked away

I don't know why I expected you to save me

I didn't care enough to save myself

The Shoe Don't Fit

It wasn't that the timing was wrong
It wasn't that I never could get the words out right
You were always a lesson wrapped in a disaster
I'm okay that you didn't turn out to be
My happily ever after

Misguided

Maybe I don't know what Love is
The only kind I cherish hurts
It whips like a storm through my life
Destroys everything in its path
Unearths my insecurities and fears
and just like that it's gone
Leaving me to rebuild and repair
No foundation, no substance
Just the better part of who I am
scattered for miles

Selfish

My mile is your inch

My 80 percent your 20

I love you with all I have

You love me with all you can give at the moment

My "I don't want you to leave"

Is your "I won't make you stay"

My "I'm at the edge of this"

Is your "I thought you were going to leave anyway"

My "I Love you"

Is your "I Love you, but I have dreams"

I guess we were both guilty of something

Trust Issues

She gave herself in small doses
so when people left it would hurt less
As relationships came and went
the doses became smaller
till she no longer felt the need to give

Thoughtless

You knew the whole time
You were just too much of a coward to say it
So you pretended, you lied
even tried to fool yourself into believing
that this was something you wanted
All the while you waited
Pined over a love you dreamed of
versus the one you had
You thought nothing of the heart
you dragged to the door
when you left to be with someone else

Never Enough

Your name is engraved in my heart
and plastered onto the broken pieces of my mind
You use me, abuse me, and I come back every time
Fed by lies, I'm not sustaining
Love is blinding
All I ever wanted you to do was fight for me
Bandages on the wounds that never healed
Too worried about how you would feel
and if you would see weakness in my pain and decide to leave

Lewis

I've seen forever in brown eyes
Tasted love's truth on full lips
I've stared at him so long he must think I'm crazy
If only he knew how long I've been searching
I'm tempted to ask "What took so long?"
It doesn't even matter now though
For I find joy in every minute, every second spent
With a man I've only dreamed of
Whom I now get to dream with

Strain

Head pounding, soul weary

She's trying to think of a happy ending

But pen to paper won't fix this

Emotions spewed out won't make this better

Words have been beaten to death

Solutions have hung themselves

Salvation

We search within lost souls
and through the lies for the truth
The unwavering absolution that someone saw us
for who we are and loved us

Discernment

These eyes have seen more pain and tribulation

than they knew they could bear

The things they wished they would have shut themselves to

Are the exact reasons they remain open

For if history is to be written

They refuse to let lies be told

Speechless

I remember nothing was quite as
frightening as the silence
The yelling I could stand
the harsh words revealed a truth
you normally were hesitant to speak
The silence though
was riddled with a heavy uncertainty
I didn't know what to say then, still don't

Gwyneth

Back against the fridge
sliding down like the tears on my face
I knew it then, I knew for a while
The empty excuses
It's like you weren't even trying anymore
One foot out the door, the other in my throat
I knew I should leave, it's just the thought of it all
left me at a loss for words
Emptier than your attempts to avoid me
A friend picked me off the floor
You were never coming
I never belonged, I lost myself trying to

New Age Love

She chases you while you chase another
All chasing some profound feeling
that none of you are prepared enough to receive
let alone nurture
This is sad; nothing is like it used to be

Confirmation

If you want something different
You have to stop accepting
what you're used to

Circles

We ignore the red flags, fall for the same lies

We see a bit of our past in our present

but convince ourselves it'll be different

We daydream that this time it'll turn out right

It all comes to a head

at the same place we've once been

Broken and confused

grasping at straws of rationalization

We love, we hurt, we lose

We forget to heal, to learn, to grow

We move forward, but we never really break the cycle

Admission

I'm trying to remember the person you were
Before the arguments, the fights
and it all went bad
I just can't
It would be fooling myself into believing
you're someone that you're not anymore

Imperfect

Every trace was erased
Each text message, photo, every handwritten note
tossed in the trash with the other sentiments
Memories aren't that easy, though, or convenient
Just when you think you have it all together
One pops right in just to remind you
of how broken you really feel

Forgiveness

I will no longer mourn the inches of me
that loved you

Fuel

I don't want to just surpass the low standards
you think I deserve
I want to completely demolish
the thought that you even had
that I was somehow less than
all based on your opinion alone
I am not angry, I'm determined
Thank you for the fuel, but the fire is all mine

The Fall

There was truth in our silence
Pain and anger in the tension
We fought to stay, fought to let go
Sometimes we just fought for the heck of it
I think we stopped knowing the difference
Then eventually we just stopped
Stopped talking
Stopped trying
Stopped caring
The only thing we didn't stop
was the other from leaving

Good Morning

I awake, my hair a mess
My limbs twisted and tangled with yours
I stop and listen to your heart beat
Thinking this is what it's all about
This is paradise
Loved devotedly, cherished deeply
and understood by this man
Who will awake and kiss me
Despite my morning breath

Transparent

I like that we have our own language
It requires no words
One look and you know what I'm thinking
I hate and love that there's no hiding who I am from you

Evolution

For too much of my life
I've apologized when I wasn't wrong
all to make a situation better
I'm not going to be that person anymore

Conformity

I feel where we fail is that we yearn
so deeply to be accepted
that we willingly give up the pieces that make us different
for fear of judgment

Trapped

Pining over loves lost
and fated to ask "what if?"
Somehow we got lost in the past
Dooming ourselves to never forget

Life of a Poet

My past looks like ripped paper and tattered notebooks

Love lost scrawled on Post-it notes

For former lovers who'll never read them

Therapy

I am thankful for all of the pieces of my heart
that got broken
It was therapeutic putting it all back together

Flatline

You're waiting for that little bit of hope
to have a lifeline
For all your patience and resilience to finally pay off
You're waiting for that person
to realize how good you are for them
Thing is, you can't force someone to see
what they don't want to

Settled

I let you mistreat me
It wasn't because I loved you
That was a lie I told both of us to justify staying
It was because I didn't love myself enough
to leave and go out and get better

Conditional Love

Change, here I was thinking I was good enough
When in truth you wanted me to be a little less like me
and a bit more like the person you pictured I could be
Funny how we love someone, flaws and all
Until the flaws start showing

Envy

The grass is always greener on the other side
When you stop watering your own

2A

My favorite color is green

I'm touching it as if it's on someone else's body

Remnants of last night are playing in my head

An accusation was made, there was yelling

It grew louder and louder

I put my hand in his face

The next moments were a haze

As if I were watching rather than living it

He punched a wall

I stood in his path when he tried to walk away from me

He gathered my things and threw them into the hall

I clung to the foot of a table

as the next thing he tried to toss out was me

He screamed in my face and then it stopped

Then came the silence

a clawing, all-encompassing quietness

I should have left

Yet here I am, lying beneath his arm, awake

The pain and green bruises proof that it wasn't a nightmare

Sadly, green is still my favorite color

Regret

To say I miss you would be an understatement
To confess every waking moment
I'm thinking about you
Would be nothing short of the truth
I must apologize because the very thing I took for granted
Is what I yearn for most now, your presence
I desire your touch, your kiss,
or even just to hear you say those beautiful three words
I didn't appreciate everything we were and now
It's all I want

Sentry

To all the women lying in bed unable to sleep

because of ghosts of past relationships or bad decisions

haunting them at night

You are not alone

You go ahead and get some rest

I'll take the first shift

Sugarcoated

I lied to myself
Edited my thoughts so
you would seem like a better man
Censored my words so
our history wouldn't seem as bleak
Weighed no more with the burden
of trying to make it right
I can admit
No, you weren't a good boyfriend
and yes, I always deserved better

Safe

Your eyes dance with a light

that captivates me to stare into your soul

Your spirit attracts me to the gates

of your heart to linger

The beat strikes a note that I respond to with an

increasing rhythm of my own

In that place, simple as it may be

I've found my home

Limbo

Some people are so stuck on who I was
that who I am never even had a chance

Standoff

Some would say I dodged a bullet

But the wounds I'm left with

would laugh in disdain

For what is a burning hole and bleeding flesh

Compared to a broken heart and shattered faith

Spring Cleaning

I'm a hoarder of memories
Crammed between how beautiful my present is
and what my past has done to me
It's not monsters that I fear but the remnants of you
that I have left under my bed
The notes, the cards, the little trinkets
I decided to clear it all out today
It's easier to look back; you already know the ending
I think it's time I actually give myself a chance
to embrace the here and now

The Chase

Some people run 'cause they want someone
to chase them
I just don't have it in me anymore to be the person
who follows behind you every time
you decide to leave

Robbed

I've had a lot of people who said they loved me
treat me like shit
I wonder which one of us
had the more fucked up definition

Dedication

She went through a snowstorm just to lie by his side
He wouldn't even walk through the rain

Exiled

I remember what you used to be like
I don't know who you are now
I wish I did
I hate the feeling that
I've been left out of your life

Stand Tall

There will be those who seek to destroy you
and everything you stand for
No matter what, keep building

Groove

It's not so much you as it is the routine
of loving you that makes it hard to quit

Distress

What is it I'm afraid of, you ask?

It is simply of losing you and in doing so losing a far

Greater part of myself

Refuge

I escape with each stroke of my pen
Each emotion that's given life on this page
I'm free
No longer left to be crushed by my inability to let go
They stay, they always stay, and I let them
They follow me from room to room
relationship to relationship
Here though, it's just me and the truth
Sometimes I don't want to leave
Just remain tucked safely in the black and white
I know once I depart I'll fall somewhere in the gray
Using my emotions and inability to cope as an excuse
not to deal with the issues
For now, I'm just going to stay here
I'm not weak, just scared
That once I clean everything up
there won't be anything left

Warrior

She goes on

Despite the fears, struggles, obstacles, and disappointments

She lives for Love of self

Love of life

And maybe one day for the Love of someone else

My Story

My words have followed me through the years
From adolescent love to the pains of womanhood
Stuffed between pages, notebooks,
in bins and book bags
Concealed within pockets of purses
Jotted-down notes in my cell phone
The passion, the agony, and ultimately, my awakening
have been there
Always hinting, always reminding
This is who I've been, who I am

Index

Andrews McMeel Publishing
a division of Andrews McMeel Universal
1130 Walnut Street, Kansas City, Missouri 64106

www.andrewsmcmeel.com

17 18 19 20 RR2 10 9 8 7 6 5 4

ISBN: 978-1-4494-8095-0

Library of Congress Control Number: 2016944684

Editor: Patty Rice
Art Director: Holly Swayne
Production Manager: Cliff Koehler
Production Editor: Erika Kuster

ATTENTION: SCHOOLS AND BUSINESSES

Andrews McMeel books are available at quantity discounts with bulk purchase
for educational, business, or sales promotional use. For information,
please e-mail the Andrews McMeel Publishing Special Sales Department:
specialsales@amuniversal.com.